Witness to History

A[...]
S[...]

David Downing

Heinemann Library
Chicago, Illinois

Produced for Heinemann Library by Discovery Books Ltd.
Photo Research by Rachel Tisdale
Originated by Dot Gradations
Printed and bound in Hong Kong, China by South China
    Printing Company

08 07 06 05 04
10 9 8 7 6 5 4 3 2 1

Library of Congress Cataloging-in-Publication Data
Downing, David, 1946-
    Apartheid / David Downing.
        p. cm. -- (Witness to history)
Includes index.
Summary: Examines the historical forces that led to the
development of
the system of apartheid, what life was like under the
system for both
blacks and whites, and the efforts that caused the end of
this system.
    ISBN 1-4034-4870-1 (HC) 1-4034-6258-5 (PB)
    1. Apartheid--South Africa--History--Juvenile literature.
2.
Anti-apartheid movements--South Africa--History--
Juvenile literature.
3. South Africa--Race relations--History--Juvenile
literature. [1.
Apartheid--South Africa--History. 2. Anti-apartheid
movements--South
Africa--History. 3. South Africa--Race relations--History.]
I. Title.
II. Series: Witness to history (Heinemann Library (Firm))
    DT1757.D68 2004
    323.168'09--dc22
                                        2003018235

Acknowledgments
The author and publishers are grateful to the following for
permission to reproduce copyright material:
Bernard Bisson/CORBIS SYGMA p. **37**; Bettmann/CORBIS
pp. **16**, **34**; Hulton-Deutsch Collection/CORBIS p. **18**; Louise
Gubb/CORBIS pp. **48**, **51**; Zen Icknow/CORBIS p. **40**; Bob
Krist/CORBIS p. **4**; Popperfotp.com pp. **5**, **6**, **9**, **11**, **13**, **17**, **23**,
26, **27**, **28**, **29**, **31**, **32**, **50**; Greg English/Reuters p. **38**;
Topham/Associated Press pp. **30**, **36**; Topham/Image Works
p. **47**; Topham Picturepoint p. **19**; David Turnley/CORBIS pp.
7, **15**, **41**, **44**, **46**; Peter Turnley/CORBIS p. **45**; UWC RIM
Mayibuye Archives pp. **20**, **24**;

Cover photograph shows a South African man taking part
in an anti-apartheid demonstration in Johannesburg in the
1950s. This picture is reproduced with permission of
Topham Picturepoint.

The publisher would like to thank Bob Rees, historian and
assistant head teacher, for his assistance in the preparation
of this book.

Every effort has been made to contact copyright holders of
any material reproduced in this book. Any omissions will
be rectified in subsequent printings if notice is given to the
publisher.

The paper used to print this book comes from sustainable
resources.

Disclaimer
All Internet addresses (URLs) given in this book were valid
at the time of going to press. However, due to the dynamic
nature of the Internet, some addresses may have changed,
or sites may have changed or ceased to exist since
publication. While the author and publisher regret any
inconvenience this may cause readers, no responsibility for
any such changes can be accepted by either the author or
the publisher.

Some words are shown in bold, **like
this.** You can find out what they mean
by looking in the glossary.

Contents

Introduction 4
How Do We Know? 6
South Africa to 1910 8
Discrimination 10
Early Opposition to White Rule 12
South Africa Adopts Apartheid 14
How Apartheid Worked 16
For Europeans Only 18
Resistance Grows 20
Sharpeville 22
A Change of Tactics 24
South Africa Is Isolated 26
Life for Whites 28
Life for Non-whites 30
The Bantustans 32
Soweto 34
The Terrorist State 36
Pressure from Inside 38
Pressure from Outside 40
First Cracks 42
The End of Apartheid 44
Reconciliation 46
Today and the Future 48
What Have We Learned from Apartheid? 50
Timeline *52*
Further Reading *53*
List of Primary Sources *53*
Glossary *54*
Index *56*

Introduction

"**Apartheid**" was the name given to the social and political system that was introduced by the South African government in 1948. "Apartheid" is an **Afrikaans** word meaning "apartness," and those who planned the system claimed that it would allow each of South Africa's major racial groups—the blacks, whites, **coloreds** (those of mixed **race)**, and Indians—to develop separately, "apart" from each other. Each group would be given their own geographical areas to live in, their own facilities to use, and their own place in the economy.

This system was put into effect by the National Party, which represented the views of most white **Afrikaners**—people who were descended from the original Dutch **colonizers** of southern Africa. Apartheid was also supported by the other major white community living in South Africa—those who were descended from British **immigrants.** In practice, this meant that the whites would have the best areas, the best facilities, and the best jobs. Apartheid had more to do with domination than separation.

How apartheid came about

White supremacy and **racial discrimination** in South Africa did not begin with apartheid—apartheid was just the last step in a

The vineyards in South Africa's western Cape Province are famous for the rugged beauty of the landscape.

process whereby European settlers gradually took control of the land and resources of the area. Over several centuries, non-whites lost most of their land to the white incomers. Basically, their country was stolen from them.

This situation was not unique to southern Africa—much the same thing was happening in Australasia (Australia,

New Zealand, and neighboring islands) and the Americas. The big difference in South Africa was that the non-white peoples always remained a large majority of the population. **Democracy** could not be introduced without threatening white control over the country's land and **natural resources.** Apartheid—and the idea of separate development—was the white community's way of dodging the issue of democracy and to make rule by the white minority look more acceptable than it really was.

Apartheid's impact

The system lasted over 40 years. It finally ended because of political, economic, and moral pressures in the early 1990s. Apartheid has an ugly history, one that is punctuated by notorious massacres of innocent people, brutal deaths in police custody, and governments which lied and deceived on a massive scale. On a daily basis black South Africans were **victimized** and humiliated. As workers they were cruelly **exploited;** members of families were often forced to live separately.

Apartheid South Africa is a good example of an independent state that disregarded the **human rights** of its own people. In the end, countries around the world got together and put real pressure on South Africa's apartheid government, but only after decades of doing good business with it. In the meantime, the country itself produced world-famous heroes like Nelson Mandela and Steve Biko, and millions of lesser known heroes and heroines who sacrificed their peace of mind, their liberty, and often their lives, to bring the system to an end.

Modern Johannesburg was founded in 1886. Its position at the heart of the Witwatersrand gold-mining region quickly turned Johannesburg into South Africa's largest city.

How Do We Know?

Walk into any bookstore or library and you will find a large section devoted to history. Look through any TV guide and you will find many programs dealing with historical events—these days there are even whole channels devoted to the exploration of the past. In a book or a film we can follow events as they happened, learn about the people involved, and learn how their actions influenced those events.

Or can we? It feels as if we are following the events and learning about the people, but in reality we are being given a historian's version of those events and people. How did the historian reach his or her conclusions? Where did he or she get the historical information from? And how much of the historian's own opinions slipped in between the lines of what he or she wrote?

Primary and secondary sources

Most histories are written many years after the events they describe. A historian may be able to study official records, personal accounts and diaries, photographs, and film. If the events took place within living memory it may even be possible to interview those who were involved. All these sources of information are called primary sources. The historian may also use books that have been written about the same events by other historians, who may have sorted and interpreted the same primary sources in a different way. Such books are called secondary sources, because the information they contain has already been through one sorting process.

Neither primary nor secondary sources can simply be taken at face value. For one thing, the record is never complete— only a small

Photographs such as this one make valuable primary sources. Here Boer General Joubert and his support staff are photographed at the beginning of the Boer War in South Africa (1899–1902).

proportion of those involved in historical events took the time to record their version of what happened and why. And those who did write personal diaries, or who did compile official records, may have tried, consciously or unconsciously, to make themselves look better and their opponents look worse. A historian has to sift through the different versions of what happened, and decide which seems most likely to be true. But a historian also has opinions and **prejudices,** and these sometimes can affect how he or she interprets both primary and secondary sources.

Telling the story of apartheid

This book tells the story of **apartheid** in two ways, through a historian's account and a wide selection of primary sources. Some of those quoted, like Nelson Mandela, took an active part in the struggle, while others, like factory worker Mandlenkosi Makhoba, played a more passive role. All the primary sources have their own points of view and their own **biases.** Some, like President de Klerk are trying to justify themselves, while others, like massacre witnesses Joshu Motha and Benedict Griffiths, are simply trying to tell what they saw with their own eyes. But no matter how biased a particular source might be, it offers a valuable contribution to the wider picture, another piece in the historical jigsaw. The more pieces we fit together, the clearer the picture becomes.

A South African man holds up his **passbook** for inspection. These passbooks, and the racial identification which they contained, were one of the cornerstones of apartheid.

South Africa to 1910

Southern Africa was first settled by black Africans several thousand years ago. The San (or Bushmen), and the Khoi-Khoi (or Hottentots), had the area to themselves until around c.e.500, when the Bantu tribes began moving in from the north. When the first Europeans arrived, around a thousand years later, there were probably more than a million native Africans living in the area.

When the Dutch established a **colony** near the site of today's Cape Town in the mid-1600s, they took land for planting their own crops and began trading with the local Africans. When the Africans protested that their land was being stolen, they were killed, forced to flee, or taken as slaves. By the end of the century the inter-mixing of the various **races** had produced a new, mixed race called **coloreds.**

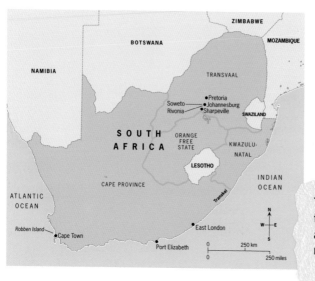

This map of South Africa shows the provinces, cities, towns, and other important places mentioned in this book.

The British seized the colony from the Dutch early in the 19th century, and from then on the white population became more equally divided between Dutch (or **Afrikaans**) and English speakers. The British rule also brought in large numbers of **immigrants** from the **Indian subcontinent.** By the end of the 19th century, the population of South Africa was approximately 67 percent black, 9 percent colored, 2 percent Indian, and 22 percent white (of whom around 60 percent were **Afrikaners**).

In the 1830s, most Afrikaners sought to escape British rule by heading off into the interior of the country on the "Great Trek."

Who came first?

This quote comes from the *Official Guide to the Voortrekker Monument*, and seeks to justify white rule. "Voortrekker" was the name given to those who undertook the Great Trek, and the monument was built to commemorate this event.

It is nonsense to suppose that the interior of Southern Africa belonged to the Bantu and that white men took it away from him. The Bantus penetrated from the north almost at the same time as the white men entered from the south. They had equal title to the country. The Voortrekkers wished to partition the country and live in peace, but the Bantu were not amenable to reason. They respected only one thing, and that was force.

A black historian's view

The following quote comes from Nthatho Motlana, a black African historian speaking on a British TV program in 1986. His comments are supported by **archaeological** evidence.

No part of South Africa can be regarded as exclusively white, nor can we accept the fact that there were large parts of our country which were empty. Our people were pastoralists who moved their herds from place to place; who ploughed land and who allowed it to be fallow if it became worked out. You cannot say to a man that this land is not yours because I did not find you at this particular place at this particular time.

A white sugar farmer sometime in the early 20th century poses for the camera while non-whites—in this case, Indians—do the work of planting his next crop.

Discrimination

Once they reached the interior of South Africa, the Voortrekkers set up two states of their own, the Transvaal and the Orange Free State. When diamonds and gold were discovered in these states in 1867 and 1886, large numbers of non-**Afrikaner** whites swarmed into them, creating a crisis which eventually led to the Boer War of 1899–1902 and the imposition of British rule throughout South Africa.

The Boer War left a feeling of resentment between the British and Afrikaners. Both communities however, knew that their political and economic position in South Africa depended on their sticking together. The settlement that led to the creation of the Union of South Africa in 1910 reflected this need for white unity. The two most influential leaders of South Africa over the next 40 years would be Jan Smuts and J. B. M. Hertzog, both of whom had led armies against the British in the Boer War.

> ## Winston Churchill speaks about the "black peril"
> This extract comes from a speech given in 1906 by Winston Churchill, then the British government's Under-Secretary for the **Colonies.** It gives a good idea of white opinion at this time, which saw non-whites as unruly children, unready to take responsibility for their own welfare. These "children" should not be treated cruelly, but neither should they be allowed to interfere with their "parents'" plans for them.

The South Africa Act, which created the Union of South Africa, stuck with the previous voting system, which allowed non-whites a small say in the election of whites in the states of Cape and Natal, and no say at all in Transvaal and the Orange Free State. The Native Land Act of 1913 divided the country's land along racial lines, allotting 92.7 percent to whites and 7.3 percent to the other **races.** Unsurprisingly, the white percentage included all the fertile agricultural land and all the known mineral wealth. The Urban Areas Act of 1923 decreed that whites and non-whites had to live in separate areas of the country's towns and cities. Long before **apartheid** was officially introduced in 1948, successive South African governments were doing all they could to separate the races and keep political and economic power in the hands of whites.

In the United States the proportion of white men to natives is eight to one and even there I believe that there are racial difficulties, but in South Africa the proportion is one white man to five natives. I ask the House to remember the gulf which separates the black man from the ancient civilization of India and China. The House must remember these things in order to appreciate how the colonists feel towards the ever-swelling sea of black humanity upon which they float. The black peril, as it is called in the current discussion of the day, is surely as grim a problem as any mind could be forced to face . . .

We will endeavour as far as we can to advance the principle of equal rights of civilised men, irrespective of colour. We will not hesitate to speak out where necessary, if any plain case of cruelty or **exploitation** of the native for the sordid profit of the white man can be proved . . .

A black miner in 1947, the year before apartheid became official policy.

Early Opposition to White Rule

The South Africa Act, and especially the refusal by whites to give non-whites greater political rights, inspired a small number of middle class blacks—doctors, lawyers, and church ministers—to form the South African Native National Congress in 1912 (the African National Congress, or ANC from 1923). This group joined similar groups representing the Indian and **colored** populations in campaigning for greater political rights. A **delegation** from the South African Native National Congress was sympathetically received in Great Britain, but the vast majority of white South Africans were not interested in listening to non-white arguments. They knew that their wealth was built on the poverty of the other **races.**

Since the ANC had failed to persuade the whites to change their ways, few blacks saw any reason to support it. Most opposition to white rule between World War I (1914–1918) and World War II (1939–1945) arose from local grievances and led to spontaneous outbreaks of violence, which were easily crushed by the white authorities.

During World War II, however, the large numbers of whites away on military duty created more openings for non-whites in important industries. Sensing their new power, these non-white workers took increasingly drastic action in pursuit of better pay and conditions, leading to the great miner's **strike** of 1946, which involved some 70,000 workers. The government managed to crush the strike by force, but white South Africans had been shown a glimpse of black South African power and they were frightened. In the elections of 1948, whites voted for a government and a system that they hoped would drive these fears away.

This was a protest meeting in a township outside Johannesburg, during the bus **boycott** of 1957. Like many such boycotts in South Africa, this one was triggered by a rise in the cost of bus fares.

Historical anecdotes from the 1957 bus boycott
The bus boycotts of the 1940s were repeated in the 1950s.
The Alexandra boycott of 1957 used the slogan "*Azikwelwa*"—
"we will not ride!" This excerpt comes from a history book
called *Organize or Starve: The History of the South African
Congress of **Trade Unions*** by Ken Luckhardt and Brenda Wall.

On 7 January 1957, workers from Johannesburg and Pretoria
townships refused to ride to work in buses owned by the Public
Utility Transport Corporation following a one penny increase in
fares effective that day. This spontaneous act of defiance marked
the start of a three-month period during which an estimated
70,000 workers boycotted the buses; amongst them, more than
20,000 African workers *each* walked a total of 3,200 kilometres
(2,000 miles).

They walked in the heat and torrential rains of a South African
summer, harassed, arrested and beaten up by the police. Women
walked, with babies on their backs and bundles of washing on
their heads.

On one occasion, two young boys were found exhausted by the
roadside after having collected a large load of washing from a
home in one of the White suburbs several miles away. Police had
apparently stopped them, accused them of stealing the washing
and drove them back to the White woman's home to find out if
they were telling the truth. After their story was confirmed, the
police officers dropped them there, forcing them to walk the 29
kilometres (18 miles) back to Alexandra all over again.

South Africa Adopts Apartheid

After World War II, it became clear that white-ruled South Africa was increasingly dependent on the non-white population to create much of its wealth. On the farms, in the mines, and in the factories, it was non-whites who did most of the hard and often dangerous work. White South Africa could not do without them, but did not know what to do with them. If non-whites were given the same political rights as whites, then the whites would lose their power, their security and, in the end, their wealth. But what was the alternative? The rest of the white world had just fought World War II against a **racist dictatorship** in Germany, and could hardly be expected to welcome a racist government in South Africa.

The solution, according to the **Afrikaner** National Party, was to separate the **races,** and to give each race control over its own territory and population. This policy was called **apartheid,** which in **Afrikaans** means "apartness." Non-white races would be allowed into white territory to work to create wealth for some of the white inhabitants, but they would only have political rights in their own territories, where the rest of their families would live in their permanent homes. This, to the whites, seemed the best solution. The territories set aside for the non-whites had nothing the whites wanted, and they could still use cheap black labor to make themselves rich. In 1948, South Africa's white population voted the National Party into power, and apartheid's half-century began.

The ruling cabinet of the National Party government in March 1951. The then prime minister, Dr. Daniel Malan (1948–54), is seated fourth from left. His successors J. G. Strydom (1954–58) and Hendrik Verwoerd (1958–66) are, respectively, seated fifth from left and standing fifth from left.

There were a number of motivations for apartheid, some
of them selfish, some **idealistic**; some admitted, some
unspoken. Foremost among these was our belief that
without apartheid our people would be swamped by the vast
black majority—and that this would inevitably lead to the
extinction of our hard-won right to national independence.
Also, we were concerned about the threat to white workers
and miners posed by competition from cheaper black labour.

There were other, more worthy, motivations: our desire that
the black cultures should be nurtured and developed and
that they should not be swamped by the more powerful
economic and technological forces of white culture.

Ultimately we feared that if blacks
and whites were to remain within
the same system they would,
sooner or later, become involved
in a struggle for supremacy that
would lead to a devastating
war between the races.

F. W. de Klerk became
the last white prime
minister of South Africa
in 1989.

How Apartheid Worked

The main point of **apartheid,** as the name suggested, was to keep the **races** apart. Over the next five years a series of laws was introduced to separate them—geographically, politically, economically, sexually, and educationally. At the same time, other laws were brought in to make sure that this separation was enforced, and that any opposition to it could be quickly and legally dealt with.

Johannesburg policemen check the passbooks of two black South Africans who have just arrived to work for six months in the nearby mines. They will not see their families during that time.

The first priority was to make sure that people were separated correctly. According to the Population and Registration Act of 1950, each person's racial group had to be established and recorded. In the absence of records this sometimes proved difficult—some people were registered as **coloreds,** for example, because a comb would not pass through their hair easily. Once established, each person's racial identity, along with their address and name of employer, was recorded on a **passbook** that had to be carried at all times.

In 1949, people of different races were forbidden to marry by the Prohibition of Mixed Marriages Act, and in 1950 the Immorality Act extended this ban to include any inter-racial sexual relationship. That same year, a new Group Areas Act clarified the existing boundaries between the areas in which each race was supposed to live, and the government started to enforce these boundaries more strictly. In 1953, the Bantu Authorities Act laid out plans for ten territorial homelands or **Bantustans,** in which the entire black population would have their permanent homes. Over the next twenty years, millions would be forced from their current homes and resettled in these homelands. There was no need to give the coloreds or Indians such homelands—their populations were not large enough to out-vote the whites.

The human cost of apartheid

The apartheid laws affected millions of individual South Africans in different ways. This account describes how one of the laws affected one family.

In 1950, just after the government introduced the Mixed Marriages Act, Raymond du Proft was serving in the police force. He was twenty when he met a waitress named Diane Bassick. They fell in love, but since she was **classified** coloured they could only meet in secret.

Du Proft remembered how scared they were that they would be found out, but before too long they took a chance and started to live together. When their first son was born they found a house in an **Afrikaans**-speaking district and passed themselves off without difficulty as a white married couple. Eventually they had five children, all of whom were classified coloured. They regularly applied for Diane and the children to be reclassified and just as regularly they were refused.

When their eldest son Graham was nineteen, he started going out with an **Afrikaner** girl and she became pregnant. As he was classified coloured, and she was white, they could not marry. His response, in a moment of despair, was to throw himself under a train. He died instantly.

This tent camp in Vyrheid, in Kwazulu-Natal province, was the new home for a thousand black South Africans evicted from their old homes under the Group Areas Act of 1950.

For Europeans Only

It was recognized that the different **races** would have to spend some time together—the white economy needed black workers, and white families needed black servants. But every attempt was made to minimize their contact. The 1953 Reservation of Separate Amenities Act laid down that parks, trains, beaches, and other public spaces would be **segregated.** Throughout South Africa signs went up—park benches marked "For Europeans only," buildings with two entrances, one marked "Whites" or *Blankes*," the other "Non-Whites" or *Nie-Blankes*."

Having separated out the non-whites, the government saw no reason to provide them with the level of education the whites took for granted. There was no use preparing black children for jobs they could never have. Also, the better educated non-whites became, the more likely they were to offer an effective opposition to **apartheid.**

Apartheid at the beach: the sign, in English and **Afrikaans,** makes it clear that this particular stretch of sand is for white use only.

To prevent opposition to its apartheid policies, the National Party brought in tougher laws against **trade union** activity in the workplace. This would prevent non-white workers from organizing themselves. Most significant of all, in 1950 it passed the Suppression of **Communism** Act, which prohibited any communist from taking part in any political activity. However, the term "communist" did not apply just to those who supported the ideas of communism as laid down by the political philosopher Karl Marx. According to the Act, a communist was anyone who "encouraged hostility" between races, who tried to bring about social or economic change through "the promotion of disorder"—anyone, in fact, who rocked the white boat.

Every expense spared

The following excerpt comes from a small book released in 1948 by the Institute of Christian-**Nationalist** Education, an influential **Afrikaner think-tank.** The ideas expressed here were used by the National Party as their justification for setting up a two-tier educational system, in which almost all the available resources were set aside for white education, and almost none for the education of non-whites.

The education of **coloureds** should be seen as a subordinate [less important] part of the Afrikaner's task of **Christianizing** the non-White races of our fatherland. Only when he is Christianized can the coloured be truly happy; and he will then be proof against foreign **ideologies** which give him an illusion of happiness but leave him in the long run unsatisfied and unhappy. He must also be a nationalist. The welfare and happiness of the coloured lies in his understanding that he belongs to a separate racial group, and in his being proud of it. Coloured education must not be financed at the expense of white education.

The white South African's duty to the native [the black South African] is to Christianize him and help him culturally. Native education should be based on the principles of looking after others, non-equality, and segregation; its aim should be to teach the white man's view of life. Native education should not be financed at the expense of white education.

This anti-apartheid demonstration took place in Johannesburg in the 1950s. Another 40 years would pass before apartheid was brought down.

Resistance Grows

The introduction of **apartheid** provoked a surge of **resistance** from the non-white population. Until the late 1940s the African National Congress (ANC) had restricted itself to argument and, occasionally, other forms of peaceful protest. But once apartheid had become state policy, the organization's Youth League—under the leadership of young men like Nelson Mandela, Walter Sisulu, and Oliver Tambo—forced through a more adventurous "Program of Action," which involved organized **boycotts**, **strikes,** and widespread **civil disobedience.** In 1951 the ANC, along with the Indian National Congress (INC), launched the Defiance Campaign, which encouraged non-whites to openly break the **segregation** and **pass laws.** Thousands were arrested and many were treated brutally in police custody.

In 1955, more than 3,000 South Africans of all **races** gathered at a Congress of the People, on the open plain just outside Johannesburg. The main organizations involved were the ANC, INC, **Colored** People's Congress (CPC) and Congress of Democrats (a new name for the **banned,** mostly white, South African **Communist** Party). Together they produced the Freedom Charter, which spelled out their agreed vision of a multi-racial South Africa.

This Charter inspired apartheid's opponents and enraged its supporters. The government's response, in 1956, was to arrest 156 leaders from the various groups, and to charge them with **treason.** Although the five-year trial ended in **acquittals** for those charged, it gave men like Mandela a platform for stating their case against the system. But they were still no nearer to ending apartheid.

As young black children try to interest a white woman in Freedom Charter leaflets, she coldly ignores them.

A different vision

This is the introduction to the Freedom Charter. Most of its demands are now taken for granted in the developed world, but it is worth remembering that very similar demands were being demanded at roughly the same time by the Civil Rights Movement in the United States.

We, the People of South Africa, declare for all our country and the world to know:

That South Africa belongs to all who live in it, black and white, and that no government can justly claim authority unless it is based on the will of all the people;

That our people have been robbed of their birthright to land, liberty and peace by a form of government founded on injustice and inequality;

That our country will never be prosperous or free until all our people live in brotherhood, enjoying equal rights and opportunities;

That only a **democratic** state, based upon the will of all the people, can secure to all their birthright without distinction of colour, race, sex or belief;

And therefore, we the people of South Africa, black and white together—equals, countrymen and brothers—adopt this Freedom Charter. And we pledge ourselves to strive together, sparing neither strength nor courage, until the democratic changes here set out have been won.

Sharpeville

The Freedom Charter produced a split in the ANC, as some blacks were suspicious of the Charter's multi-racial message. They wanted to gain their freedom without any help from whites, no matter how well intentioned, and left to form the black-only Pan-African Congress (PAC). It was the PAC that organized a demonstration against the **pass laws** in the small town of Sharpeville on March 21, 1960.

Some 5,000 unarmed protesters gathered in front of the local police station and refused police orders to leave. Eventually, for reasons that remain unclear, the police panicked and opened fire on the demonstrators, killing 69 and wounding a further 180 people. Most of these were shot in the back as they tried to escape.

The opposition groups ordered a national stay-at-home day in protest, and organized a march through the white areas of Cape Town. For a few days it seemed as if the National Party government, now led by Hendrik Verwoerd, had lost its nerve—the pass laws were temporarily suspended and there were even promises of talks with black leaders. But then, just as suddenly, the government swung in the opposite direction. A **state of emergency** was declared, 18,000 people were arrested, and the ANC and PAC were both **banned.**

> **Benedict Griffiths and Joshu Motha answer questions on the Sharpeville massacre**
> These excerpts come from the questioning of Benedict Griffiths, the seventeen year-old son of a black police officer, and Joshu Motha, a black bus driver, at the Court of Enquiry into the Sharpeville massacre. The Court found that the police were not to blame.

The Sharpeville massacre proved to be a turning point in two important ways. It showed the rest of the world how brutal **apartheid** was and forced the National Party government to choose between two alternatives—reform or increasing isolation from the rest of the world. It chose the latter. Second, the Sharpeville massacre convinced black opposition groups that peaceful change was not possible. They decided, reluctantly, to take up arms.

After the massacre at Sharpeville in 1960, white policemen wander through the strewn bodies of the black protesters whom they and their colleagues have killed.

Question: I want to come back to the time just before the shooting started. Was it your impression, then, that the crowd was trying to attack the police?

Griffiths: No.

Question: What was the crowd like imediately before the shooting?

Griffiths: They were happy and they were singing.

Question: Did you see anybody near where you were, throwing stones at the police?

Griffiths: No, I did not see one.

Question: You heard someone shout "Skiet!" ["Fire!"], and then what happened?

Motha: I did not get frightened at all. I thought it was only blank cartridges that they were firing. At that time, I was facing towards the gate . . . As I turned I saw a male, non-European, lying on the ground . . . Just at that time, I felt a bullet grazing my trousers—it did not go in—on my right leg. The trousers were torn. Then I got fright. I thought to myself "Hah! Are they shooting real bullets?" Just as I lifted my left leg to go forward, I was struck by a bullet here, in the right hip, and I dropped.

A Change of Tactics

In the months that followed the **banning** of the ANC and PAC, both organizations set up their own armed groups. These were called Umkhonto we Sizwe (Spear of the Nation) and Poqo (Pure) respectively. These groups had no hope of fighting a successful **guerrilla war** in the near future—they had few men or weapons, whereas the South African army was well equipped and efficient. In addition, most of the countryside was far too open for successful guerrilla warfare, with few hiding places from which to conduct ambushes or sudden attacks.

The first aim of the armed groups was to mount an occasional, and hopefully newsworthy, operation against the state. The PAC had no objection to killing whites, particularly those working for the government, but the ANC, true to its long tradition of peaceful protest, concentrated on industrial and military targets.

Their campaigns failed, at least in these early years. A few people were killed, a few electricity generators blown up, but the state was not threatened. Black leaders like Nelson Mandela were permanently on the run from the security forces. In 1962 Mandela was caught, and a few weeks later other leading ANC members, Walter Sisulu, Govan Mbeki, Ahmed Kathrada, Elias Motsoaledi, and others—were arrested at their secret headquarters in Rivonia, a country suburb of Johannesburg. They—and particularly Mandela—used their trial (October 1963–June 1964) to publicize their cause, but all were given long sentences. The ANC had been badly weakened, and black South Africans had lost their most important political leaders.

These are the "Rivonia 8," all of whom were sentenced to life imprisonment in 1964. Clockwise from top left: Nelson Mandela, Walter Sisulu, Govan Mbeki (father of the current president), Raymond Mhalaba, Dennis Goldberg, Ahmed Kathrada, Andrew Mlangeni, and Elias Motsoaledi.

A call to arms

On December 16, 1961, five explosions in Johannesburg and five in Port Elizabeth marked the beginning of Umkhonto we Sizwe's armed struggle against the government. At the same time, posters were distributed with the following message.

Umkhonto we Sizwe is a new, independent body formed by Africans. It includes in its ranks South Africans of all **races.** Umkhonto we Sizwe will carry on the struggle for freedom and **democracy** by new methods which are necessary to complement the actions of the established national liberation organizations ...

It is, however, well known that the main national liberation organizations in this country have consistently followed a policy of non-violence. They have conducted themselves peaceably at all times, regardless of government attacks and persecutions upon them, and despite all government-inspired attempts to provoke them to violence ... But the people's patience is not endless.

The time comes in the life of any nation when there remain only two choices: submit or fight. That time has now come to South Africa. We shall not submit and we have no choice but to hit back by all means within our power in defence of our people, our future and our freedom.

South Africa Is Isolated

Sending the political leaders of South Africa's black population to jail made the white government feel safer, but it also enraged many people around the world. The ANC, realizing how important support from other countries might be, established a permanent mission abroad under Oliver Tambo. This mission established contacts with the anti-**apartheid** groups that were springing up in many countries. The South African government met world criticism with defiance. When the British **Commonwealth** threatened to expel South Africa, the government simply announced it was leaving anyway. The country was declared a **republic,** and all political links to the British monarchy and Great Britain were broken.

Oliver Tambo is explaining events in far-off South Africa to a London audience in 1976. For almost 40 years Tambo was the ANC's ambassador to the world. He died in 1993.

South Africa's increasing isolation was most obvious in the field of sport. When the government refused, in 1965 and 1968, to allow New Zealand and England to include non-white players in touring rugby and cricket teams, huge international arguments broke out, and from 1968 on South Africa was banned from the Olympic Games.

International sportspeople, forbidden to compete in South Africa, often argued, with some justice, that they were the only people who were being asked to make a real sacrifice in the struggle against apartheid. **Western** businesses were attracted by South Africa's cheap labor and mineral wealth (i.e. gold), and their investment in the country, far from shrinking, grew steadily through the 1950s and 1960s. Partly as a result of this, South Africa enjoyed one of the world's highest economic growth rates during this period. As far as the white government was concerned, apartheid was working.

Basil D'Oliveira remembers

Basil D'Oliveira was a good enough cricketer to play for South Africa, but could not do so because he was **colored.** He eventually moved to—and played for—England. In this excerpt he remembers playing and watching the game as a youth in **segregated** Cape Town.

Although we coloureds had little to do with white people, I eventually wanted to find out more about their style of play and facilities. Whenever possible I'd go to Newlands, Cape Town's famous stadium, to watch the great white players in Test matches. I'd look at the lush outfield and the beautiful wicket and wonder what it would be like to play here, and not in my usual park, where about twenty different games were going on at once. I longed to play here, if only for one day. But that was one dream I was never allowed to realize.

Colored cricketer Basil D'Oliveira was denied the opportunity to play for South Africa, and ended up playing for England instead. His selection for the England team to tour South Africa in 1968–1969 led to the cancellation of the tour, and South Africa's exclusion from world cricket.

Film censorship

White South African author Brian Bunting tells how films were affected by the **censorship** laws.

Sometimes censorship went beyond the bounds of all sense. Scenes featuring the famous **African-American** trumpeter Louis Armstrong were taken out of the film *The Glen Miller Story*, although advertisements containing his name appeared all over the country. The advertising posters for [the musical] *The King and I* were designed to show Deborah Kerr embraced by a bare-chested Yul Brynner in the role of the Siamese King. Since Siamese are Asians, however, this could not be allowed, and the posters were altered to reveal Deborah Kerr in the arms of a raceless shadow.

Life for Whites

When **apartheid** was at its strongest, from the early 1950s to the mid-1970s, most South African whites enjoyed an extremely high standard of living. The system had originally been introduced, at least in part, to save the jobs of poor whites from black competition, and the number of poor whites declined rapidly during these years. In 1971 the average white wage was 21 times the average black wage.

The vast majority of whites lived in good houses in well-kept areas, enjoying excellent education, health care, and leisure facilities. Many employed servants.

This luxury mansion in a white area of Johannesburg is typical of the lifestyle that apartheid was supposed to preserve.

Some whites were unwilling to enjoy the benefits of a system that relied so clearly on the **exploitation** of other racial groups. Many of these people left the country, most of them **emigrating** to other parts of the white world, like Great Britain, Australia, or North America. Some stayed to fight the system in whatever way they could, as courageous journalists, outspoken churchmen, secret **communists**, troublesome members of **parliament**, and even rock stars.

Most white South Africans, though, did support apartheid. This was partly because they did not want to see South Africa dominated by the country's black majority, and partly because the system gave them such a high standard of living.

Johnny Clegg's song of opposition
For many years Johnny Clegg has led a mixed **race** band in South Africa singing songs of rebellion in both English and **Zulu.** This song is about looking forward to the end of apartheid.

Dr. Jakobus Steyn speaks

Dr. Jakobus Steyn was one of many whites interviewed in the early 1980s by journalist Victor Crapanzano for his book, *Waiting: The Whites of South Africa*. Here he explains that, like many whites, he would never be able to cope with black rule.

Time is running out for the white man. If we don't take a stand together, then we'll go under. We must take a very firm stand towards the Coloured and the Black. We are prepared to share the country—territorial **segregation**—as we have done with the homelands. We're prepared to do that. But I'm not prepared to let my culture go by letting these people take over. If they are going to take over, the majority, then I'll leave. I'll never be able to sit here and be ruled by the Black man.

We're on our way home to
    find our freedom,
And I'm on my way home to
    find you my friend,
Where we can stand in
    the light of the people
And breathe life into the
    land again.
Siyathemba, siyathemba
    kuwena nkosi,
(We are hoping and we
    still believe,)
Sizofika emakhaya,
(We will reach our final
    destination,)
Ngizobeka phansi uku zondama
    kwami,
(I will put down my hatred,)
Ngizobeka phansi izenzo
    zegazi,
(I will lay down my acts of
    revenge,)

Johnny Clegg, the "White Zulu," and other members of Savuka perform in Johannesburg in January 1990, a month before the release of Nelson Mandela.

Ngizoxolelana nezitha zami
    wemadoda,
(I will forgive my enemies,)
Sizofika emakhaya
(We will reach our final
    destination).

29

Life for Non-whites

During this period, life for the non-white **races**—the blacks, **coloreds,** and Indians—was very difficult. South Africa's non-whites lived in a rich country, but were denied anything like a fair share of the wealth they worked to create. In both town and country, they mostly lived in poor housing. What educational, health, and leisure facilities they had were usually poor and always inferior to those enjoyed by the whites.

People employed in the cities as servants or **service workers** often had to make long journeys into work from the **townships** that ringed the white cities. Men employed in the mines and factories usually worked long hours for little pay, in dangerous conditions, and spent what leisure and sleeping hours they had in dirty and crowded **hostels.** Since these men were forbidden to bring their families with them, they often saw their wives and children for only a few days each year. Having no political rights, and only the most limited **trade union** rights, there was nothing they could do to change this situation.

In the countryside, non-whites had to scrape a living from the poorest agricultural land, send their children to schools that lacked books and equipment, and travel great distances to receive the most basic health care. Wherever they worked or lived, non-whites were continually reminded of their second-class status by arrogant police behavior and by the poor public facilities provided for them. Those who protested were beaten, or put in jail without trial, or both.

This woman and her children live in a corrugated metal home in one of the black townships that ringed the white cities.

Mandlenkosi Makhoba writes about his experiences as a factory worker

Most ordinary black South Africans living under **apartheid** had neither the time, the energy, nor the education to keep a record of their day-to-day lives. This source is taken from a short book written by a young factory worker, Mandlenkosi Makhoba, who was determined to tell his story.

For the sake of my family I was forced to leave home. I left when I was a young man to work in the factories far away. I first set foot in Johannesburg in 1959.

Two gold miners share a meal in their hostel, sitting on the open boxes that also serve as their beds.

Vostoorus Hostel is one of the many badly built and badly kept hostels which are part of our lives. They are small and cramped for so many people. The hard stone floors are cold in winter. The rooms have no ceilings. They are hot in summer. And the hostels are far from town.

We are forced to work long hours and wait in queues [lines] for buses which often do not arrive. We came here to work for our families, but it is the white man who gets rich, and it is us who have done all the work. I know because I have seen this town grow. I have worked hard for twenty years but have nothing in my hands. The wealth we have created has been stolen by the bosses. They and their families are rich, but we have to live in hostels while our families suffer.

31

The Bantustans

There was one glaring contradiction at the heart of **apartheid.** The system was supposed to separate the **races,** to allow them to develop apart from each other. The economy, however, which produced a high standard of living for the whites, was completely dependent on non-white labor to function. Economically, the races could not be separated.

The tribal homelands, or **Bantustans,** were the National Party's way of separating the races politically without destroying the economic link. These ten homelands—one for each of the ten major tribes recognized by the government—were intended, eventually, to be independent states inside the borders of South Africa. All blacks would have their official homes in one of these states, and would only be allowed into white South Africa as guest workers. This was basically a scheme for making black South Africans foreigners in their own country. They would have political rights in the Bantustans but, like foreigners anywhere, would have only limited rights in "foreign" white South Africa. The whites would still have their cheap workforce, but would be able to claim that they had no responsibility for the housing, education, health care, or political rights of the workers.

The first Bantustans were given self-government in the early 1970s, and in 1976 Transkei became the first to be granted "independence." None of these "states" ever received international recognition, and most South African blacks saw them for what they were, just another ploy for extending white dominance.

This woman is left with her possessions after being moved to a resettlement area in one of the homelands in 1984.

Cosmas Desmond reports on the homelands

In the mid-1960s, priest Cosmas Desmond saw his black parishioners forcibly removed from their homes for resettlement in a Bantustan. Shocked by the conditions they were forced to endure, Desmond made it his business to visit other homelands and report on what he found. Here he describes a new settlement at Rietspruit in the western Transvaal.

No sanitation was provided and very few had built their own latrines [toilets]. There was one well for water, about a mile from some parts of the settlement, serving all the people— whenever I went there, there was a fairly long queue [line]. There were no shops at all; travelling salesmen visit the area and there are shops in a village about two miles away. There was no clinic or resident nurse; a government health inspector visits once a week and deals with cases of malnutrition. The school was temporarily housed in tin huts; two years after the first people arrived the new school building had only reached window height. A few one-roomed houses had been provided for old people; some were brick under asbestos, others were all corrugated iron.

When I visited Rietspruit again a couple of months later some of the shacks had started to fall apart. More people had arrived, some of whom were still in tents, others in temporary shacks. One shack was made entirely of old plastic fertilizer bags. The settlement, bad as it was before, had deteriorated still further.

Soweto

The early 1970s were bad years for **apartheid.** The South African economy was badly affected by the world oil price rises of 1973–1974, which led to higher prices in the stores, rising unemployment, and a wave of **strikes** by black workers. In 1974, Portugal finally gave independence to two of South Africa's northern neighbors, Angola and Mozambique, and their new governments allowed the ANC and PAC to set up bases just across the border.

Inside South Africa, the ANC and PAC were still **banned** and because their leaders were still in prison it was hard for them to gather support or exert influence. In the early 1970s the **Black Consciousness** Movement rose to prominence. This movement stressed the need for blacks—a word now used to cover all non-whites—to liberate themselves. It was influenced by African thinkers like Franz Fanon and by **African-American** movements in the U.S. In South Africa, its most important spokesperson was Steve Biko.

The ideas of this movement gained popularity in the few black universities, and in schools, particularly those in the huge **townships** that ringed the white cities. When, in the winter of 1976, the government insisted that math be taught in **Afrikaans,** schoolchildren organized protest marches. One of these, in the township of Soweto on June 16, ended with the police opening fire. At least twenty children were killed. Over the next year protest followed protest, and around 600 people lost their lives. One of them was Steve Biko, who was beaten to death by the police.

One schoolgirl's story

In the days that followed the June 16 children's march in Soweto, the whole area erupted in violence. Priscilla Msesenyane was one of thousands caught up in these terrifying events.

During the day further incidents of unrest broke out. We heard gunshots from the direction of the Esso Garage and we rushed there to see what was happening. Trucks were stopped and looted, and police fired shots in an attempt to disperse the crowd. As the crowd was scattered, my aunt was shot, but we could not stop to find out how she was.

I ran home and hid under a van parked in our yard. The Boers [Afrikaners] came into the yard, carrying guns. They grabbed some of the people who ran into our yard. I stayed under the truck, quietly, until they left. I stayed there until I was certain they were gone. By the time I came out, I could smell tear-gas fumes in the air. I was terrified that the Boers would beat me up like they did those they grabbed in our yard.

When I emerged from under the van, things had quietened down a bit. I quickly ran into the house where I locked myself in. Peeping through the windows, I could see police in armoured trucks chasing people and beating them up.

Black schoolchildren and college students rioted in Soweto on June 16, 1976. These riots triggered months of serious violence throughout the country, and some historians believe that the apartheid government was never again in complete control of the country.

The Terrorist State

Steve Biko was the 46th black person to die in police custody in little over a year. South Africa was now a police state—a state in which the police considered themselves above the law. Most of the children who died in the disturbances of 1976–1977 were shot by the police, but very little was done by politicians or the police themselves to investigate the circumstances, let alone bring the guilty to justice.

Steve Biko formed the People's Convention, a political group that aimed to raise **black consciousness.** He was beaten to death while in police custody in 1977.

Since the early 1960s, the laws of arrest had been continually altered to help the police. In 1962 they could arrest and hold someone on suspicion for up to 12 days; in 1963 this was extended to 90 days and in 1965 to 180 days. In 1966, indefinite detention was allowed only if authorized by a judge, but in 1976 even the need for authorization was dropped. The police could now arrest and hold someone, without trial, for as long as they wanted, merely because they suspected him or her of actively opposing the government.

Once in jail, suspects were likely to be tortured. Many were killed. The police reports of the time were full of claims that prisoners had fallen down stairs or leapt from windows to their deaths.

Finding people to arrest was not difficult. For one thing, the police employed a huge web of informers, both inside and outside the country, to bring them information on real or potential rebels. For another, most non-whites hated the system under which they were forced to live, and would have said so at one time or another.

Brutality in police custody

This is how a small black African newsletter told the story of one black African arrested in the summer of 1962–1963. At least W. Bongco survived his ordeal.

One night the police woke up W. Bongco at his home and after searching him at his house took him to the police station, where they used strong-arm tactics to get information about the firearms [weapons] they were searching for. They handcuffed him and hung him up against the wall. They then assaulted him, some using sjamboks [whips] . . . Bongco fell unconscious and they untied him. When he recovered they trampled and kicked him with their boots, using obscene language. They were mad with anger, some crying and shouting that if he continued to be stubborn they would take him to the bush and shoot him dead and say he was trying to escape. At this time blood was already oozing from their victim's ears. After some rest they resumed their work and, squeezing him by the neck, gave him hard blows which rendered him partly deaf. He went unconscious again and this time they took him to shower his clothes and washed him before they could release him . . . Today Bongco is in bed at the local hospital as a result of his beating by the police.

Riot police stand guard outside Cape Town University, September 1985. South African police were well-equipped to crush those who openly protested against **apartheid**.

Pressure from Inside

Despite the huge power of the **apartheid** state, opposition to it continued to grow. After the protests in Soweto, there was no return to peace, as there had been after Sharpeville. There were raids across the border by ANC fighters based in Angola and Mozambique, and a rapid growth of small organizations campaigning on different issues, like housing costs, education, youth facilities, and health care. In 1983 several hundred of these organizations came together as the United Democratic Front (UDF), which began holding mass meetings and pushing, as the ANC had back in the 1950s, for peaceful change. The government refused to listen, and through 1984–1985 increasingly violent disturbances shook most of the major towns and cities.

Black **trade union** activity also grew, mainly because of a change in the importance of black workers to the South African economy. Since the 1960s, that economy had branched out into the sort of sophisticated industries that needed a flexible and well-educated workforce. Because there were not enough whites to do all the new jobs, some of them had to be done by blacks. That meant better education for blacks and, as a result, blacks who were better able to bargain to demand better pay and living conditions. Apartheid's attempt to separate the **races** was getting ever more difficult.

Mourners carry 27 coffins to their place of burial in April 1985. All had been shot dead by police during riots in Uitenhage, near Port Elizabeth.

Defiance from ANC prisoners

Walter Sisulu, along with Nelson Mandela and other members of the ANC, was imprisoned on Robben Island. This excerpt from Walter Sisulu's book, published in 2001, gives an account of how prisoners on the island refused to be beaten down by their white captors.

We knew that the Island was no ordinary prison. Its main aim was to punish and **demoralize**. Right from the start the authorities were clear—the purpose was to break our morale and destroy any political ideas we might have. When a **political prisoner** goes to jail, he tells himself he will not allow himself to go under. We decided that we would always speak as a group and through a leader, and from almost the very beginning Nelson [Mandela] was that leader. We forced the warders and prison authorities to talk to us through him, although they tried to break that up over and over again. But we stood together, and they failed.

Defiance from Steve Biko

Steve Biko, who was killed while in police custody in 1977, had always emphasized how important it was for black South Africans to speak out against apartheid.

Our belief is that white society will not listen to preaching. They will not listen to their **liberals**. Liberalism has not grown within white society, and we blacks cannot stand idly by watching the situation. We can only generate a response from white society when we, as blacks, speak with a black voice and say what we want. Now has come the time when we, as blacks, must articulate [say] what we want, and put it across to the white man, and from a position of strength.

Pressure from Outside

While political and economic pressures were eating away at **apartheid's** foundations inside South Africa, the regime was also facing increasing difficulties in its dealings with the outside world. With each new cycle of violent protest and state repression—from Sharpeville to Soweto to the bloody disorders of the mid-1980s—world condemnation grew louder and more sustained. By this time almost all sporting contacts had been ended, and the strong feelings felt by ordinary people around the world against apartheid were finally affecting the relationship between **Western** business and South Africa.

African-American anger at the situation in South Africa was also making itself felt, and in August 1985 U.S. banks stopped lending money to South Africa. Over the next couple of years, more campaigns were launched against U.S. business involvement in that country. Faced with a choice between losing customers at home or closing down their South African operations, more than 70 U.S. companies, including Kodak and General Motors, withdrew from South Africa.

White South Africa had no friends left, and there were increasing calls for the sort of hard-hitting **economic sanctions** which might finally bring apartheid down. These, however, were still resisted by the West, often with the excuse that they would hurt black South Africans more than white South Africans.

This rally in support of the ANC in London in 1990 was organized by the Anti-Apartheid Movement, which had enjoyed worldwide support since the 1960s.

The case against sanctions

Many in the West, like British prime minister Margaret Thatcher, wanted to avoid sanctions. This excerpt comes from Thatcher's autobiography, published in 1995.

I pointed out just how damaging sanctions and disinvestment were to those we were allegedly trying to help. I gave the example of an Australian firm which had just closed a fish-canning factory near Cape Town putting 120 non-whites out of jobs. I noted that a general ban on fruit and vegetable exports would destroy between 10,000 and 20,000 non-white jobs—and all those affected would have no **social security benefits** to fall back on.

The case for sanctions

Desmond Tutu, then Archbishop of Cape Town and an outspoken critic of apartheid, made the following response to such arguments in 1986. Tutu, however, always opposed the use of violence. He was awarded the Nobel Prize for peace in 1984.

The argument that the blacks would be the first to suffer may be true yet there are at least two answers to it: a cynical one is, when did whites become so unselfish? After all, they have benefited from black misery engendered by low wages, migrant labour, etc., for so long. The less cynical is that blacks would probably be ready to accept suffering that had a goal and a purpose and would therefore end, rather than continue suffering endlessly.

Desmond Tutu addresses a meeting in the **township** of Alexandra, outside Johannesburg, in 1986, the year in which he became Archbishop of Cape Town.

41

First Cracks

When P. W. Botha succeeded B. J. Vorster as prime minister of South Africa in 1978, he announced that **apartheid** had to "adapt or die." Over the next decade he tried to adapt it through a series of reforms. He hoped these reforms would be strong enough to win international acceptability and peace at home, but not so hard-hitting that they threatened white control over the economy and political system.

Botha's government increased the share of the country's wealth which was spent on the black population, putting more money into black education and improving **township** life by providing more people with electricity and running water. In the mid-1980s some apartheid laws—like the **pass laws** and the Immorality Act—were scrapped, and plans were announced to give the **colored** and Indian populations their own elected **parliaments.** The black majority was not promised any new political rights, but black **trade unions** were given some powers, and black-run local authorities became more directly responsible for black areas.

This attempt to save apartheid by reforming proved unsuccessful. Most non-whites saw the attempt for what it was, and refused to have any part of it. Few coloreds or Indians voted for their new parliaments, and those blacks who accepted white offers of minor jobs often found that their own people despised them for it. During the violent disturbances of 1984–1985 many were killed for "**collaborating** with the enemy."

Police use horsewhips to discourage demonstrators from marching on Nelson Mandela's prison in 1985.

Nelson Mandela speaks from prison

By the mid-1980s the PAC had declined in importance, but the ANC, which had absorbed most of the **black consciousness** and UDF activists, had gone from strength to strength. In 1985 President Botha tried to improve his regime's image by offering the ANC leader Nelson Mandela his freedom, but only on the condition that the ANC abandon its campaign of violence against apartheid. This is part of Mandela's reply.

I cherish my freedom dearly, but I care even more for your [the people's] freedom. Too many have died since I went to prison. Too many have suffered for the love of freedom.

I owe it to their widows, to their orphans, to their mothers and their fathers who have wept for them. Not only I have suffered during these long lonely wasted years. I am no less life-loving than you are; but I cannot sell the birthright of the people to be free. I am in prison as a representative of the people and your organization, the African National Congress, which was **banned**. What freedom am I being offered while the organization of the people remains banned? What freedom am I being offered when my very South African **citizenship** is not respected. Only free men can negotiate. Prisoners cannot enter into contracts. I cannot and will not give any undertaking at a time when I and you, the people, are not free. Your freedom and mine cannot be separated.

The End of Apartheid

In 1989, illness forced Prime Minister Botha to step aside in favor of F. W. de Klerk. This change of leader signaled a change of tactics from the National Party government, which finally accepted that **apartheid** was doomed. The white authorities set out to strike a bargain with those who spoke for the black population, and the first step was to release them from jail. On February 11, 1990, Nelson Mandela took the short walk to freedom in front of the world's TV cameras. He had been in prison for 27 years.

The bargain which the National Party struck with the ANC was simple. In exchange for the blacks gaining political power in a one person, one vote **democratic** South Africa, the whites would be allowed to keep their economic power. The apartheid state would be pulled down, but there would be no immediate seizure of white property or industry.

The Inkatha Movement, unlike the ANC, was based on a single ethnic group—the Zulus.

The details of this bargain, and the new political system which it made possible, took several years to work out. In the meantime, the main apartheid laws were repealed. During these years many thousands lost their lives in incidents of violence, some involving extremist whites, but most caused by differences among the blacks. The most bitter of these feuds was fought out in Kwazulu-Natal between the ANC, which claimed to represent all South Africans, and Chief Buthelezi's Inkatha Party, which claimed that only it could represent the **Zulus.**

The first democratic elections were eventually held in 1994, and the ANC, as expected, won a huge majority. Nelson Mandela became South Africa's first black president, and vowed to create a rainbow nation from the country's different colors and cultures.

Free at last

On February 12, 1990 *The Times* (an English newspaper), like most newspapers around the world, led its front page with the release of Nelson Mandela. In this passage, the paper's South African correspondent captures the excitement of the moment.

The Times

12 February 1990

Mr Mandela first appeared at the gates of Victor Verster Prison at Paarl, 40 miles from Cape Town, at 4.14 p.m. local time – more than an hour behind schedule. Holding his wife Winnie's hand and repeatedly punching the air in a victory salute, he tried to walk a few yards, but was halted by the crush of thousands of ecstatic supporters who had waited hours in searing sunshine to welcome him.

With a smile and a wave Mr Mandela climbed into the silver BMW sedan and drove off escorted by four police motorcycle riders. In the pandemonium in Cape Town, the motorcade apparently took a wrong direction and missed the rear entrance to the City Hall, which had to be cordoned off. The car was immediately engulfed by a seething, screaming mass of humanity, which trapped it for 15 minutes.

Outside the City Hall, a vast crowd waving green, black and gold banners of the African National Congress gathered to hear Mr Mandela. He told them that 'our struggle has reached a decisive moment. Our march to freedom is irresistible.'

In April 1994, villagers in Nelson Mandela's birthplace line up for their first-ever chance to vote.

Reconciliation

The decades of **apartheid,** and the centuries of **racial discrimination** which had preceded it, were bound to leave a legacy of bitterness and resentment. Many crimes had been committed by the white state and its employees, both inside and outside the prisons.

Mandela and the other ANC leaders recognized the need for an investigation, but feared that a campaign of revenge, no matter how legal, would make racial peace that much harder to achieve in the new South Africa. They decided instead to set up a Truth and **Reconciliation** Commission (TRC). Those guilty of crimes would be invited to explain themselves, to tell their stories, and in return they would be forgiven for whatever it was they had done. Archbishop Desmond Tutu was made chairman of this new commission.

Nelson Mandela is shown here at his presidential inauguration ceremony in 1994. During his speech Mandela spoke about the need for reconciliation.

The commission's hearings went on for several years, a long and painful tale of man's inhumanity to man. It had its critics: some South Africans—like Steve Biko's family, for example—were angry that those who had killed their loved ones got off free after admitting their guilt. And some prominent people who refused to appear before the commission—like ex-Prime Minister Botha and Chief Buthelezi—were never forced to answer the charges against them. But overall, the TRC did perform a useful role in uncovering the truth of what had happened in the apartheid years, and in forcing the white community to face the fact that many cruelties had been committed in their name.

F. W. de Klerk addresses the Truth and Reconciliation Commission

This is an excerpt from F. W. de Klerk's opening remarks when he addressed the commission.

I stand before you today, neither in shame nor in arrogance, but deeply conscious of my responsibility to admit that which was wrong, to defend that which was right, and to continue to build bridges in our quest for reconciliation; my responsibility to help formulate a framework for a peaceful future for all South Africans.

Policeman Jeffrey Benzieh, a known torturer of **political prisoners**, pleads for forgiveness and amnesty at the Truth and Reconciliation Commission.

Desmond Tutu's feelings

In this passage, Chairman Desmond Tutu expresses his feelings after hearing weeks of often harrowing testimony at the Truth and Reconciliation Commission.

I have recently presided over the first round of hearings of the **Human Rights** Violations Committee of the Truth and Reconciliation Commission. We thought we knew the extent of suffering that our people underwent during the dark days of apartheid's repression. But most of us have been quite devastated by the depth of depravity and evil which has been revealed in testimony after testimony. By rights the stuffing should have been knocked out of our people by the atrocities committed against them. And yet it has not been so. We have often been humbled and deeply touched by the nobility and generosity of spirit of those who despite so much pain and anguish, have amazed the world by their willingness to forgive the perpetrators of all these dastardly deeds of darkness.

47

Today and the Future

After serving one five-year term, Nelson Mandela stepped down from the presidency at the age of 80. In the elections of 1999 the ANC were again victorious, and Thabo Mbeki took over as president. South African **democracy** was obviously working.

However, the country still has major problems. More than a decade after Mandela's release, South Africa remains a highly unequal country in which one minority racial group—the whites—still holds most of the economic power. The lack of any dramatic change in this regard has, of course, encouraged whites to stay. And this in turn has promoted economic stability and encouraged outside investors to put their money in South Africa.

But that same lack of change has angered many black South Africans. They argue that not enough resources are being put into black health care, black education and training, black housing, and leisure facilities. They say that the government—their government—is not redistributing South Africa's wealth fast enough. They believe that other social evils—like the huge rise in crime and the **AIDS** epidemic sweeping the country—cannot be effectively tackled until something is done about poverty.

All these problems could have been foreseen in 1990—transforming a **racist dictatorship** into a multi-racial democracy was never going to be quick or easy. Yet in many ways it is remarkable just how far South Africa has come in little over a decade, and how distant the era of **apartheid** already seems.

A young mother keeps watch over her sick daughter, one of South Africa's many AIDS victims. She had already lost a four-year-old son to the disease.

Chris McGreal writes

The end of apartheid raised enormous expectations among the black majority. A decade later, in his last report from South Africa, *Guardian* (an English newspaper) journalist Chris McGreal gave a pessimistic assessment of how much the ANC government had done to meet those expectations.

The Guardian

1 November 2002

In 1994, when the ANC came to power, the World Bank characterised South Africa as a country marred by 'destitution among plenty'. The poorest 10 per cent of South Africa's population share a smaller slice of the pie now than they did when apartheid ended, and jobs are harder to come by than at any time for decades. South Africans were shocked to learn earlier this month that children still starve to death in the eastern Cape and Kwazulu-Natal.

Shortly before he became president, Thabo Mbeki told parliament that South Africa was two nations – one white, the other black; one rich with every opportunity laid before it, the other theoretically equal, but in practice denied the same opportunities. Four years later, Mbeki still oversees two nations in South Africa, but now they are divided by class. Whites command a smaller share of the pie, but the benefits have not been widely distributed among non-white South Africans. Instead, a new black elite [privileged group] has been created. Racial equality has come to mean no more than the right of a few black leaders to become as rich as the white minority.

What Have We Learned from Apartheid?

By the middle of the 20th century, it was already obvious to a lot of people that the rule of one **race** over others was morally unacceptable, but **apartheid** made it more obvious to more people. The indignities, brutalities, and stupidity of a system that offered rewards according to skin color were exposed, over a 40-year period, for the whole world to see.

Apartheid taught the world another important lesson—that those who wish for racial domination find it harder and harder to say so. Hitler's Nazis openly admitted their ambition to rule and exploit other races, but after their defeat in World War II, others with similar intentions grew more careful with their language. The architects of apartheid wanted domination, but they talked of "separate development." It is often useful to hear what governments say, but it is always crucial to watch what they do.

For the rest of the world, apartheid South Africa was a lesson in how a government should not treat its own people. Sports **boycotts** irritated many white South Africans, but it was only real economic pressure, worldwide disapproval, and growing violent protests that forced the apartheid regime to reform and finally disband itself.

Unfortunately, apartheid also offered new proof of how badly human beings can treat each other. Mindful of this, the leaders of the new South Africa set out to teach the world a new lesson, of how well those same human beings can learn to live together.

This is new housing in Sebokeng, some 40 miles (64 kilometers) south of Johannesburg. In 2000, South Africa still needed around three million more homes.

The new South Africa: a multi-racial group of Cape Town students sit and chat on the grass outside the university, May 1999.

Nelson Mandela explains what kept him going

The story of apartheid is interwoven with the story of its most famous enemy, Nelson Mandela. Here he explains what kept him going through the long years of imprisonment, and why he expects so much of the new, post-apartheid South Africa.

I never lost hope that this great transformation would occur. Not only because of the great heroes of our time, but because of the courage of the ordinary men and women of my country. I always knew that deep down in every human heart, there was mercy and generosity. No one is born hating another person because of the colour of his skin, or his background, or his religion. People must learn to hate, and if they can learn to hate, they can be taught to love, for love comes more naturally to the human heart than its opposite. Even in the grimmest times in prison, when my comrades and I were pushed to our limits, I would see a glimmer of humanity in one of the guards, perhaps just for a second, but it was enough to reassure me and keep me going. Man's goodness is a flame that can be hidden but never extinguished.

Timeline

8000B.C.E.	Southern Africa occupied by black San and Khoi-Khoi tribes
to 1500	Slow spread into southern Africa of black Bantu tribes
1652	First Dutch **colony** established in southern Africa
1806	British take control of European settled areas (the Cape and Natal)
1836	Dutch Boers—the "Voortrekkers"—migrate north to escape British rule in the "Great Trek"
1899–1902	The Boer War
1910	Union of South Africa created
1912	South African Native National Congress (later the African National Congress or ANC) is formed
1913	Native Land Act sets aside seven percent of South Africa's land for the black population
1914–18	World War I
1923	Natives (Urban Areas) Act divides South Africa's towns and cities into white and non-white areas
1939–45	World War II
1946	Black mineworkers' **strike**
1948	National Party under Dr. Malan wins the **"apartheid** election"
1950–53	Main apartheid laws introduced
1952	ANC leads "Defiance Campaign"
1955	Freedom Charter presents an alternative vision for South Africa
1958	PAC (Pan-African Congress) splits from ANC
1960	Sharpeville massacre; ANC and PAC **banned**
1961	South Africa leaves **Commonwealth** and becomes a **republic;** ANC and PAC begin armed struggle
1963	Rivonia Trial opens in October
1964	At Rivonia Trial, Nelson Mandela and other ANC leaders are sent to prison for life
1966	B. J. Vorster becomes prime minister
1968–71	Beginnings of **Black Consciousness** Movement
1976	Student protests in Soweto trigger a year of unrest in the **townships;** Transkei becomes first 'independent' black homeland
1977	Steve Biko murdered in police custody
1978	P. W. Botha becomes prime minister
1983	Introduction of Indian and **colored parliaments**
1984–86	Large-scale unrest, leading to the proclamation of a **state of emergency**
1986	**Pass laws** abolished
1987	Many U.S. companies pull out of South Africa
1989	F. W. de Klerk succeeds Botha as prime minister
1990	Mandela released and ANC unbanned
1991–94	Remaining apartheid laws abolished; continuing violence, particularly between ANC and **Zulu** Inkatha in Kwazulu-Natal
1994	ANC wins first **democratic** elections; Mandela becomes president
1999	Mandela steps down; Thabo Mbeki becomes president

Further Reading

Connolly, Sean. *Apartheid in South Africa.* Chicago: Raintree, 2003.

Cooper, Adrian. *Racism.* Chicago: Raintree, 2003.

Gogerly, Liz. *Nelson Mandela.* Chicago: Heinemann Library, 2003.

Tames, Richard. *The End of Apartheid: A New South Africa.* Chicago: Heinemann Library, 2000.

List of Primary Sources

The author and publisher gratefully acknowledge the following publications from which written sources in the book are drawn. In some cases the wording or sentence structure has been simplified to make the material more appropriate for a school readership.

p. 9: *Official Guide to Voortrekker Monument;* Nthatho Motlana, speaking on Granada TV's *Apartheid* series in 1986.
p. 11: Winston Churchill: *A History of South Africa*, Martin Roberts (Longman, 1990).
p. 13: *Organize or Starve: The History of the South African Congress of Trade Unions*, Ken Luckhardt & Brenda Wall (Lawrence and Wishart, 1980)..
p. 15: F. W. de Klerk: *The Last Trek – A New Beginning*, (Macmillan, 1998).
p. 17: From David Harrison's research for the BBC program, *The White Tribe of Africa*, (1981).
p. 19: *The Rise of the South African Reich*, Brian Bunting (Penguin, 1964).
p. 21: *Apartheid, The Facts*, (IDAF, 1991).
p. 23: *Shooting at Sharpeville*, Ambrose Reeves, Archbishop of Johannesburg (Victor Gollancz, 1966).
p. 25: *The Rise of the South African Reich*, Brian Bunting (Penguin, 1964).
p. 27: Basil D'Oliveira: *Time to Declare*, (Dent, 1980);
   The Rise of the South African Reich, Brian Bunting (Penguin, 1964).
p. 29: Dr. Jakobus Steyn: *Waiting: The Whites of South Africa*, Vincent Crapanzano (Granada, 1985);
   Johnny Clegg and Savuka: "When The System Has Fallen," *Heat, Dust & Dreams*, (EMI, 1993).
p. 31: Mandlenkosi Makhoba: *The Sun Shall Rise for the Workers*, (Ravan, 1984).
p. 33: Cosmas Desmond: *The Discarded People*, (Penguin African Library, 1971).
p. 35: Elsabe Brink, Gandhi Malungane, Steve Lebelo, Dumisani Ntshangale, Sue Krige, *Soweto, June 16, 1976*, (Kwela, 2001).
p. 37: *The Rise of the South African Reich*, Brian Bunting (Penguin, 1964).
p. 39: Walter Sisulu: *I will go singing*, (Waterfront, 2001);
   A History of South Africa, Frank Welsh (HarperCollins, 1998).
p. 41: Margaret Thatcher: *The Downing Street Years*, (Harper Collins, 1995).
   Desmond Tutu: *South Africa Since 1948*, Jean Hayward (Wayland, 1989).

p. 43: Nelson Mandela: *South Africa*, Ian Phillips (Holmes McDougall, 1989).

p. 45: *A History of South Africa*, Frank Welsh (HarperCollins, 1998).

p. 47: Desmond Tutu: his preface to *I Write What I Like*, Steve Biko (Bowerdean, 1996); British Library monograph YA1997b5784

p. 49: Chris McGreal: "The Shame of the New South Africa" *Guardian*, November 1, 2002.

p. 51: Nelson Mandela: *Long Walk to Freedom*, (Abacus, 1995).

Glossary

acquittal   declaration of innocence

African American   black American whose ancestors were brought to the United States from Africa as slaves

Afrikaans   language spoken by Afrikaners

Afrikaner   white South African with Dutch ancestors

AIDS   life-threatening disease transmitted through bodily fluids

apartheid   system of segregation and discrimination in South Africa that forced whites and blacks to live apart from each other

archaeology   study of human history and prehistory by looking at the sites and remains of human settlement and other physical artifacts

banned   (for political party) forbidden to operate

Bantustan   area set aside for black people within South Africa to remove them from white areas

bias   usually an unfair feeling for or against someone, thing, or group

black consciousness   being aware and proud of one's identity as a black person. Also a term given to the movement in South Africa and the United States to promote such feelings.

boycott   refusal to have dealings with a business firm or institution

censorship   controlling what information the public can and cannot read, hear, or see

Christianize   turn into a Christian

citizenship   having the rights and responsibilities of a citizen

civil disobedience   peaceful form of protesting usually involving the refusal to obey particular laws

classified   put into a particular grouping

collaborate   work together

colonizer   person involved in the colonization of a country or region

colony   (usually poor) country ruled by another (usually richer) country

coloreds   in South Africa, people of mixed race

Commonwealth   group of independent countries once ruled by the United Kingdom that now promote economic and cultural links among themselves

communism   originally an extreme form of socialism, in which property is held in common, rather than individually. In South Africa the word was used to describe anyone who opposed the apartheid system

delegation   group of people who represent and act on the wishes of others

democracy   political system in which governments are regularly elected by the people

demoralize   make someone feel bad about himself or herself

economic sanctions   measures, such as a stoppage of trade, that are used to persuade a country to change its policies

emigration   leaving your own country to live permanently in another

exploitation   making use of, often unfairly or selfishly

guerrilla war   war fought on one side by unofficial and irregular troops, who tend to rely on surprise, hit-and-run attacks

hostel in South Africa, a place for workers to stay

human rights rights that should belong to any person

idealistic believing that the world can be made a better place

ideology set of inter-connected social, political, and economic ideas

immigrant person coming in from another country to live

Indian subcontinent countries of India, Pakistan, and Bangladesh

liberal in apartheid South Africa, person who hoped to bring about change through argument and persuasion

nationalist someone who actively promotes the interest of his or her nation

natural resource material that is found in nature, like gold or oil, that can be used and sold to bring wealth to a region or country

nurture help to grow

parliament law-making assembly which has been at least partly elected

passbook document containing owner's racial identity, address, and employment details

pass laws laws that limited the movement of blacks within South Africa

political prisoner someone imprisoned for his or her political beliefs

prejudice fixed opinions that are held without taking account of the facts

race large group of people with similar physical characteristics, like color of skin and hair, that differs from those of other groups of people

racism hostility toward people of other races

racial discrimination treating people differently because they belong to a particular racial group

racist dictatorship political system in which one race has total control over others

reconciliation restoration of harmony after a period of conflict

republic state without a king or queen, where the leaders are usually elected or nominated by the people

resistance fighting back

segregation in racial matters, the enforced separation of races

service worker person involved in jobs that provide services to others and not in manufacturing goods, i.e. a bus driver

social security benefits payments made by the government to people who have no work or are unable to work

state of emergency description of situation by a government which allows it increased powers to detain people or to keep them off the streets

strike stoppage of work by employees in order to press for changes in pay or working conditions

think-tank group set up to explore possible policies

township small town or area of a South African city set aside for black housing

trade union organization formed to protect and advance the pay and conditions of workers

treason crime against the government or ruler of a country

victimize make a victim of someone by punishing them unfairly

West/Western term used to describe the industrialized nations of western Europe, North America, Australia, and New Zealand

white supremacy rule of white people over other peoples, and the belief held by some whites that the white race is superior to other races

Zulu large, black ethnic group of people living mainly in Kwazulu-Natal province

Index

Afrikaners 4, 8–9, 10, 14
AIDS 48
ANC (African National Congress) 22, 26,
  34, 38, 39, 40, 43, 46, 48, 49
  formation of 12
  and Youth League 20
  and Umkhonto we Sizwe 24
  bargain with National Party 44
anti-apartheid demonstrations 19, 20,
  22-23, 34–35, 38, 40, 42

Bantu Authorities Act 16
Biko, Steve 5, 34, 36, 39, 46
Black Consciousness Movement 34, 36, 43
Boer War 6, 10
Botha, P. W. 42, 43, 44, 46
bus boycotts 12–13
Buthelezi, Chief 44, 46

censorship 27
Churchill, Winston 10–11
Civil Rights Movement (U.S.) 21
Clegg, Johnny 28–29
Congress of Democrats 20
Congress of the People 20
CPC (Colored People's Congress) 20

Defiance Campaign 20
D'Oliveira, Basil 27

education 18–19, 28, 30, 34, 38, 42, 48
elections (1994) 44, 45

Freedom Charter 20–21, 22

Group Areas Act 16, 17

Immorality Act 16, 42
INC (Indian National Congress) 20
Inkatha movement 44

Klerk, F. W. de 7, 15, 44, 47

Mandela, Nelson 5, 20, 24, 39, 42, 43, 44–45,
  46, 48, 51
Mbeki, Thabo 48, 49
mines and factory workers 11, 12, 14, 16,
  30–31

National Party 4, 14, 18, 19, 22, 32, 44
Native Land Act (1913) 10

Olympic Games (1968) 26
Orange Free State 10

PAC (Pan African Congress) 22, 24, 34
passbooks 7, 16
pass laws 16, 20, 22, 42
police brutality 36–37
Population and Registration Act 16
Prohibition of Mixed Marriages Act 16, 17

Reservation of Separate Amenities Act 18
Rivonia trial 24
Robben Island 39

sanctions 40–41
Sharpeville massacre 22–23
Sisulu, Walter 20, 24, 39
South Africa
  becomes a republic 26
  British rule 8, 10
  business and wealth 26, 27, 28, 40
  early history 8–9
South Africa Act 10, 12
sports boycotts 26, 40, 50
Suppression of Communism Act 18

Tambo, Oliver 20, 26
Thatcher, Margaret 41
townships 30, 34, 42
trade unions 18, 30, 38, 42
Transvaal 10
tribal homelands (Bantustans) 16, 32–33
Truth and Reconciliation Commission
  46–47
Tutu, Desmond 41, 46, 47

Union of South Africa 10
UDF (United Democratic Front) 38, 43
Urban Areas Act 10

Verwoerd, Hendrik 22
Voortrekkers 9

World Wars I and II 12, 14, 50